S HARMONY

basic terms

by
Cecily Dell

Revised by
Aileen Crow

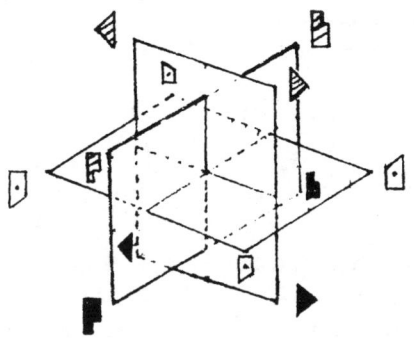

Revised 1977 by
Irmgard Bartenieff

NEW YORK 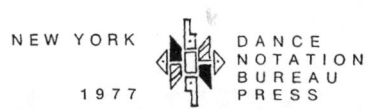 DANCE
NOTATION
BUREAU
1977 PRESS

2

Printed in the United States of America

by

Dance Notation Bureau, Inc
19 Union Square West
New York, New York 10003

Second Printing, January 1975
Third printing, December 1977

Cecily Dell (1966
Aileen Crow (rev. 1969)
Irmgard Bartenieff (rev. 1977)

SPACE HARMONY

Basic Terms

GENERAL TERMS USEFUL IN SPACE HARMONY

POSTURAL - Active flow of movement through-
out the whole body in a consist-
ent manner - In contrast to
movement of only a part of the
body; arms, head or trunk alone.

SHAPING - Shaping is movement involving
constantly changing three dimensional relationships of the
body to space. Anatomically
shaping requires a combination
of rotation, extension or flex-
ion, and ad or abduction in the
torso, limbs and head. The
opposite of maintaining a static
shape or position, shaping
refers to the quality of sculpt-
ing 3 dimensional forms in
space.

GATHERING & SCATTERING - general shaping
coming toward the body or going
away from it, not specific about
where in space.

CENTRAL - Movement which is initiated from
or passes through the center of
the body. The dimensional scale,
the diagonal scale and the diameters (plane diagonals) of each
plane are central movements.

4

diameters of sagittal plane   🝾 ▮ 🝾 ▮

horizontal plane   ◖ ◗ ◢ ◣

vertical plane   ▷ ◀   ◁ ▶

PERIPHERAL - Movement occuring in the
outer limits of one's kinesphere, usually initiated by
the extremities. Peripheral
refers to movements which
follow the edges of the icosahedron, or which connect the
extremes of the dimensional
or diagonal crosses. The primary scales, the girdles, the
(peripheral) three-rings, and
the five rings are peripheral,
as are the connecting paths
between transversals in the
two-rings, e.g.,

(icosahedron)   (octahedron)   (cube)

▷ ◖ ▮ ◀ ◗   ◢ ▷ ◖ ▮   ◢ ◗

(icosahedron)   (octahedron)   (cube)

TRANSVERSE - Movement which passes between
the body center and the periphery
of the kinesphere.

SPACE/EFFORT AFFINITIES: The assoc-
iation of specific Efforts or Effort
combinations with specific spatial
paths.

eading from the right side of the body, the
ffinities are:

- ▨ upward movements with ($\mathcal{V}$) lightness
- ▮ downward movements with ($\int$) strength
- ▐ forward movements with (_$\diagup$) slowness
- ▐ backward movements with ($\diagdown$) quickness
- ◁ sideacross movements with ($\frown$)directness
- ▷ side open movements with ($\diagdown$)indirectness

——— SPATIAL FORMS AND SCALES ———

KINESPHERE - The area surrounding the body
within the reaching possibilities
of the limbs without changing one's
place. It is usually related to
postural movement which emphasizes
the space around one, in contrast to
general space in which action and
locomotion takes place.

DIMENSIONAL CROSS - The orientation of the
body (in space) with three axes:
vertical (up-down), horizontal
(side-side), sagittal (forward-
backward). These axes lie per-
pendicular to one another, and
intersect at a point which coin-
cides with the center of the
body. (The center of gravity is
directly below this spatial
center.)

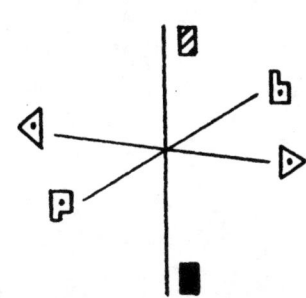

DIMENSIONAL SCALE - A sequence of six
            one-dimensional movements along
            the cross of axes, originating
            from and returning to the center
            of the cross (body center) as it
            describes a pathway through the six
            available directions.

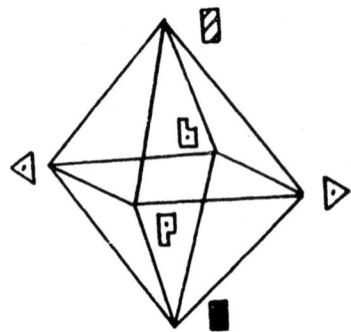

OCTAHEDRON - Geometric model established
            by connecting the extreme
            reaches of the six directions
            of the dimensional cross.

Movement along the edges of this
model is peripheral. Such movement allows transitions from one
dimension to another without
going out of the Octahedron.

example:

It is also possible to alternate
central and peripheral movements
in the octahedron.

example: ▷ ▨ ▯ ▯ ◁ ▯ ▮ ▯

THE THREE PLANES - The extension of the
dimensional cross into planes:
the vertical (or door) plane including the dimensions up-down
and side side divides the space
in back; 2) the horizontal (or
table) plane including the dimensions side-side and forward-
backward divides the space of
the upper body from that of the
lower; 3) the sagittal (or wheel)
plane including the dimensions
forward-backward and up-down
divides the space on the right
side of the body from that on
the left.

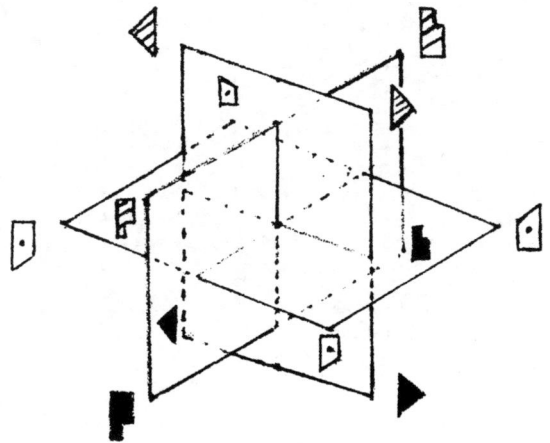

DIAGONAL CROSS - There are four full diagonals, passing through the center of the body and extending
into space, remaining equally
distant from each of the three
planes. They stress equally three
movement tendencies: vertical,
horizontal and sagittal. The
diagonals are:

high right forward to deep left backward

high left forward to deep right backward

high left backward to deep right forward

high right backward to deep left forward

CUBE - The geometric model established by
connecting the extreme reaches of
the eight directions of the diagonal cross.

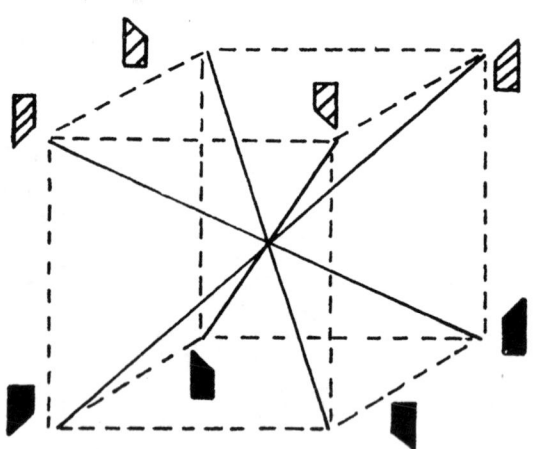

DIAGONAL SCALE - The scale composed of the
     eight directions of the diagonal
     cross. Each movement in one of
     the eight diagonal directions is a
     central movement with three spatial
     tendencies of equal importance,
     thus primarily a shaping movement
     in character. These alternate
     with 2 dimensional peripheral move-
     ments along the surface of the
     cube:

ICOSAHEDRON - When the corners of the three
     planes are connected, they form
     an icosahedron, a geometric model
     from which various spatial scales
     and forms can be explored. A trans-
     ition from one plane to another
     results in a modified diagonal
     pathway with three unequally
     stressed spatial tendencies. One
     can go peripherally along the
     edges or transversely inside the
     model. Traveling from point to
     point inside the cube or octa-
     hedron produces central movement.
     In the icosahedron it produces
     transverse movement unless one
     stays in the same plane in a
     diameter of that plane. All the
     scales and variations of the
     icosahedron involve movement
     with three spatial tendencies
     which are never of equal impor-
     tance. Complex three dimen-
     sional gradations and variations
     in movement are possible using
     the icosahedron as a model.

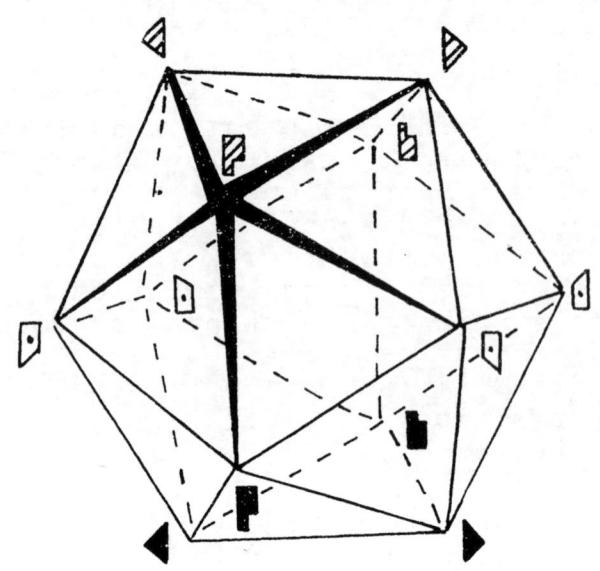

TRANSVERSALS: - Diagonally inclined, with uneven stress on three spatial tensions, these movements occur between the corner of two planes passing through a third and progressing inside the icosahedron. Each of the four full diagonals produces six related trans-versals in the icosahedron. Two are modified by stressing width, the ◁▷ dimension, two by stressing height, the ▎ dimension, and two by stressing depth, the 𝄐 dimension.

example:
for diagonal

the flat ◁▷ variations are: and

the steep ▎ variations are: and

the suspended variations are: and

FLAT - The quality of a transverse inclination that moves from the <u>horizontal</u>
to the <u>vertical</u> plane in the icosahedron. It is produced because the
two planes share a side/side
component.

STEEP - The quality of a transverse inclination that moves from the vertical
plane to the sagittal plane. It
is produced because the two planes
share an up/down component.

SUSPENDED - The quality of a transverse inclination that moves from the
<u>sagittal</u> to the <u>horizontal</u> plane.
It is produced because the two
planes share a forward/backward
component.

INCLINATION - A transversal movement which is
deflected from the diagonal toward
either vertical, sagittal, or horizontal axes of the cross of axes.
Also called modified diagonal.

AXIS SCALE - The scale covering all possible
transversals related to the same
diagonal, maintaining the order of
transition from one plane to another
as flat, steep, suspended. There
is one axis scale around each of
the four diagonals.

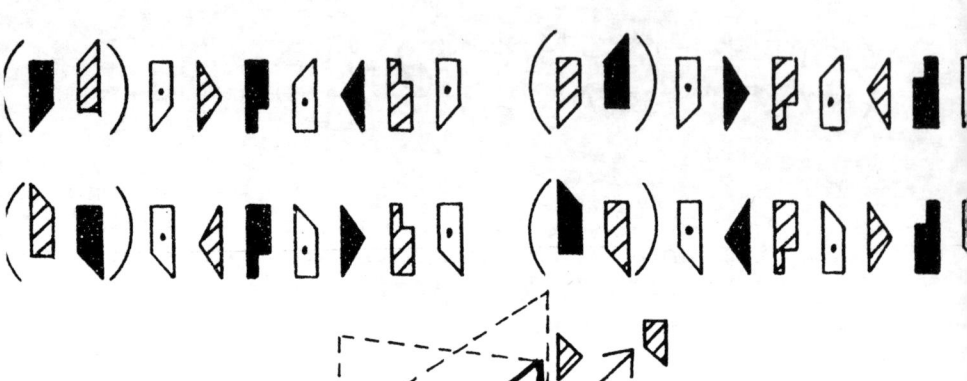

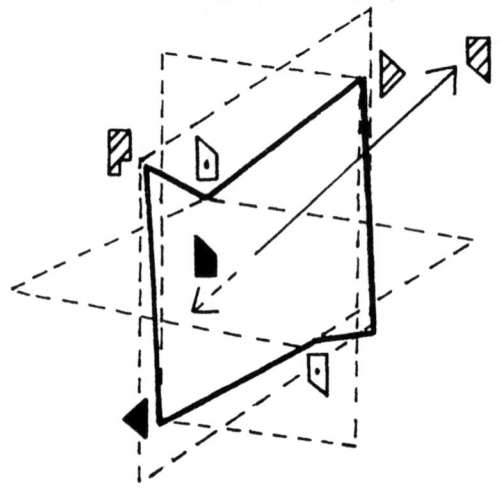

See p. 16
Choreutic

PRIMARY SCALE - A sequence derived from the
   Axis Scale. It consists of 12
   peripheral inclinations around the
   same diagonal as the six transversals of the Axis Scale. There is
   one primary scale based on each of
   the full diagonals.

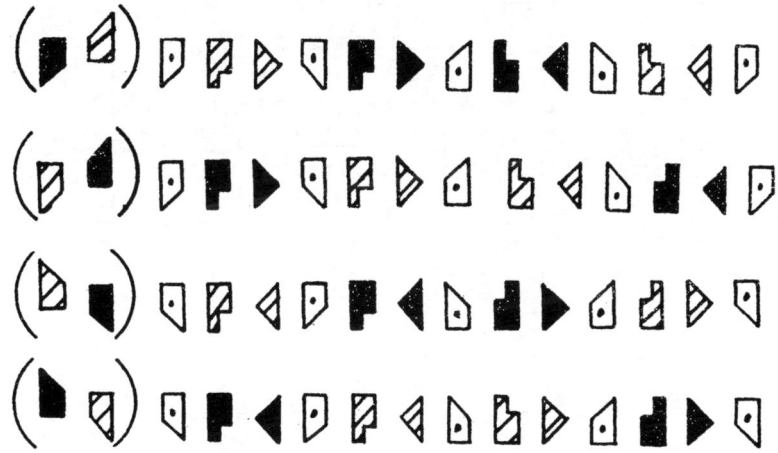

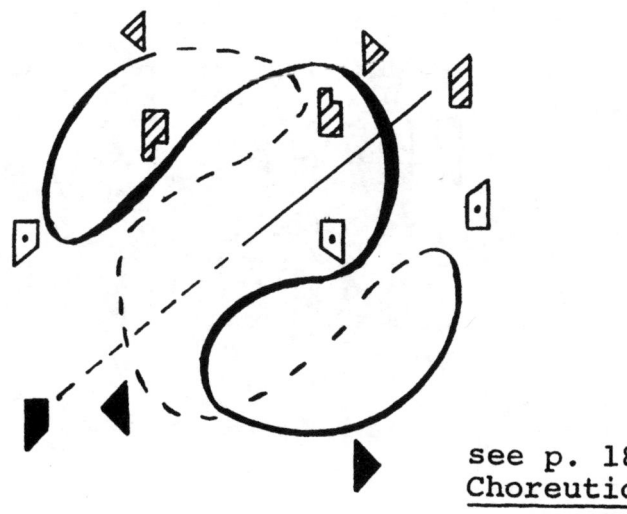

see p. 180
Choreutics

14

TRANSVERSAL SCALES (A & B SCALES) - A Scale:
        a sequence within the icosahedron
        that consists of twelve transversal
        inclinations touching the twelve
        corners of the three planes of the
        icosahedron. The inclinations are
        from the three diagonals; the se-
        quence moves around the fourth.
        The order is from vertical to
        sagittal to horizontal planes four
        times and the inclinations con-
        sequently appear as flat, steep,
        suspended. The B Scale mirrors
        the A Scale. There are right and
        left A Scales and right and left
        B Scales.

Axis
(left out)

Right A Scale

Axis
(left out)

Left A Scale

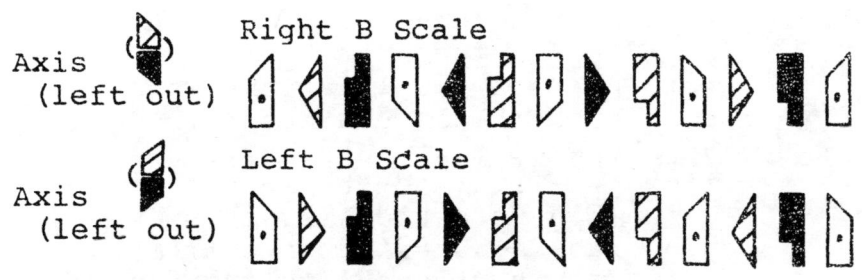

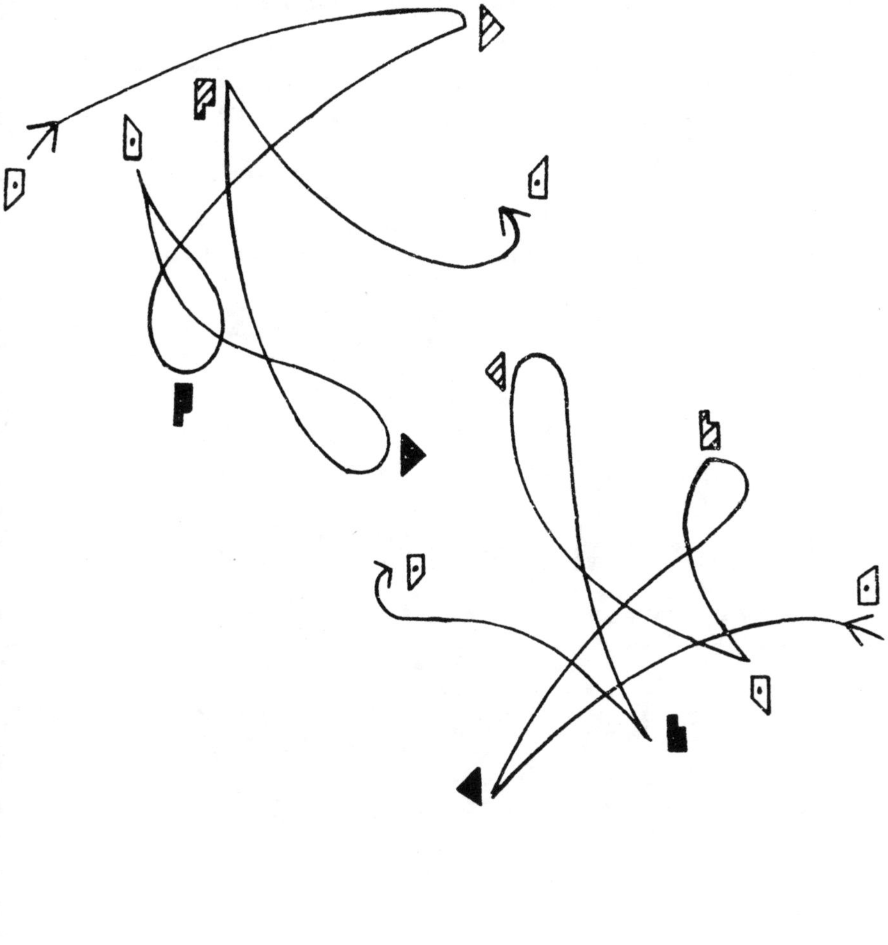

Right B Scale

Left B Scale

1st and 2nd halves of Right A Scale

STEEPLES - Angular movements produced by
           dividing up the A or B scales
           into pairs of inclinations which
           emphasize the same diagonal. Since
           no shape elements are carried over
           from the first to the second in-
           clination in a steeple, the move-
           ment has an abrupt change from the
           first to the second inclination.

           Steeples in the Right A scale show-
           ing the diagonal emphasized:

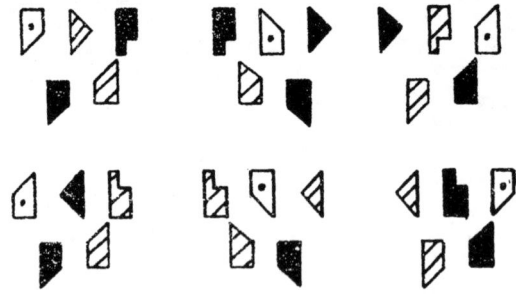

           Steeples in the Right B scale show-
           ing the diagonals emphasized.

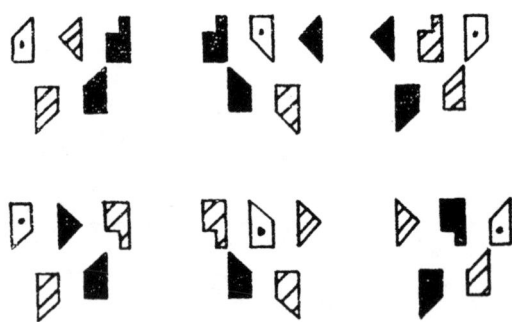

VOLUTES - The large, curved movements produced by dividing up the A or B
scales into pairs of transverse
inclinations in which the diagonal
of the first inclination is
different from that of the second.
The weakest spatial tendency in
the first inclination is carried
over to the second inclination
becoming its second strongest
tendency. The carry-over of this
one spatial tendency produces a
continuity of form (absent in
the steeples). If one performs
the volutes according to the dy-
namics produced by the effort
affinities of the spatial tendencies, one experiences a cres-
cendo of one effort element and
a weaker and stronger emphasis in
the other two.

Volutes in Right A scale with
shape and effort emphasis:

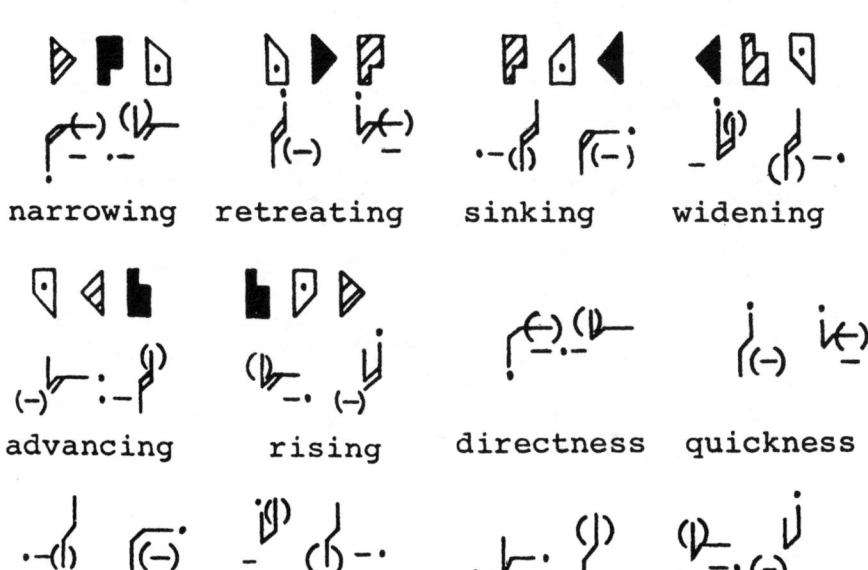

narrowing   retreating   sinking   widening

advancing   rising   directness   quickness

strength   indirectness   slowness   lightness

Volutes in Right B scale with
shape and effort emphasis:

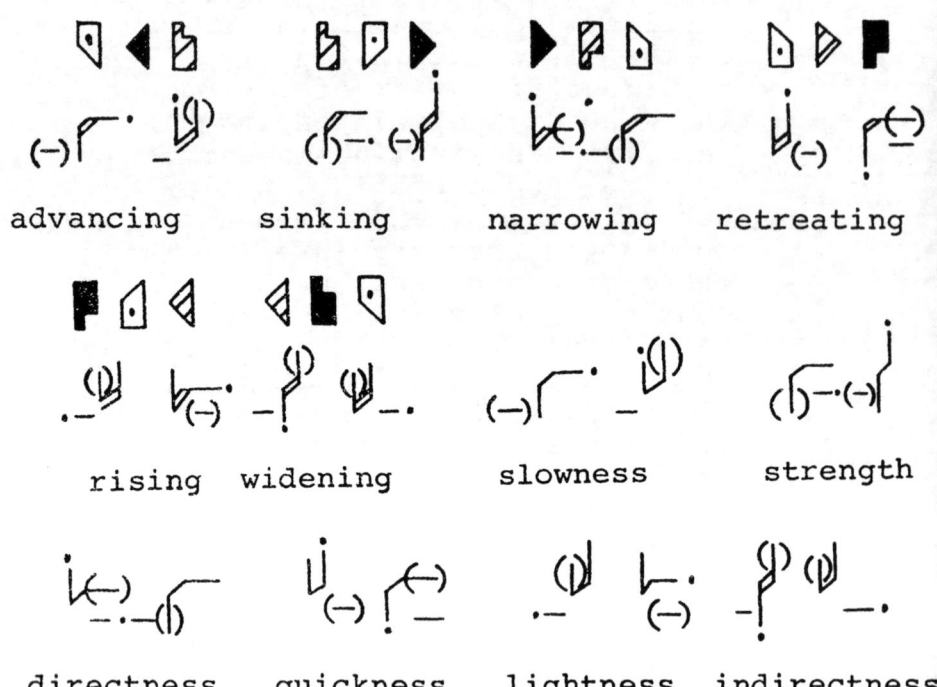

advancing   sinking   narrowing   retreating

rising   widening   slowness   strength

directness   quickness   lightness   indirectness

RING -   Any movement sequence that
travels a complete circuit.

GIRDLE - A circuit of 6 peripheral inclinations around each of the
4 diagonals. This is not a
plane, but a 3 dimensional shape
formed by the zig zag surface
lines encircling the icosahedron.

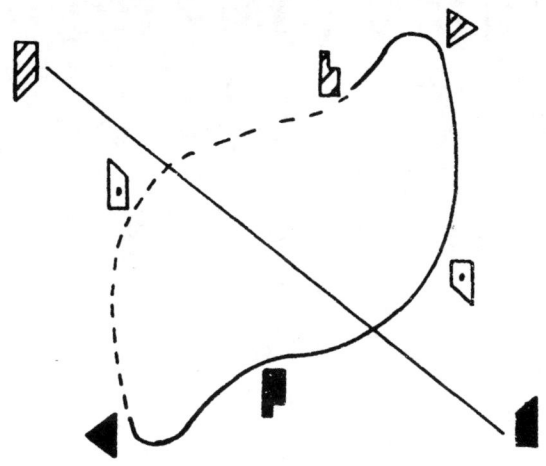

TWO-RING - In the icosahedron, two parallel transverse inclinations
alternating with two parallel
peripheral inclinations (i.e.,
peripheral-transverse-peripheral-
transverse) forming a plane.
Three two-rings can be built
using the parallel transversals
derived from each of the four
diagonals: one will consist of
two flat inclinations, one of
two steep inclinations, and
one of two suspended inclinations.

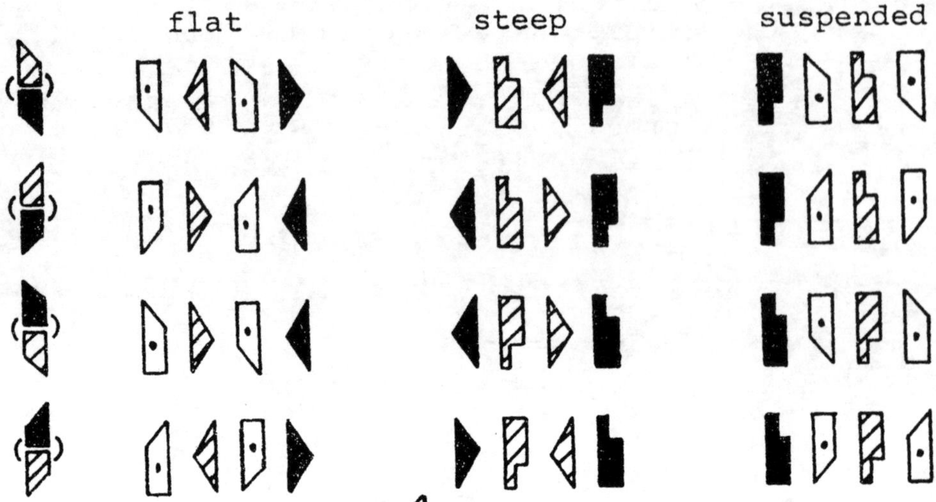

flat   steep   suspended

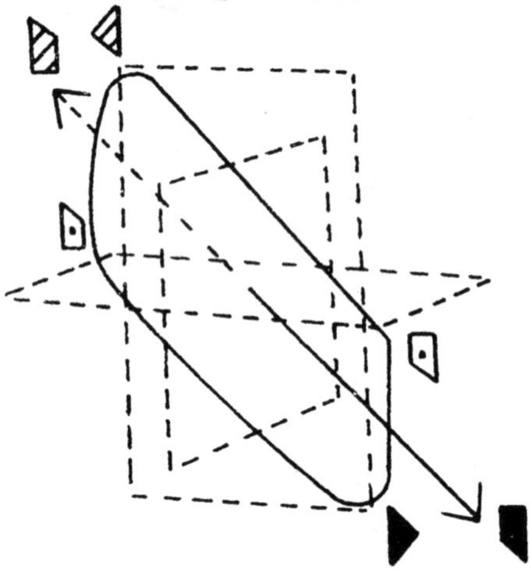

a flat 2-ring
derived from

THREE-RING - In the icosahedron, a circuit
made up of either three transverse or three peripheral inclinations. Two transverse and two
peripheral three-rings are
possible around each full diagonal (making eight of each). A
transverse three-ring involves
three different diagonals. Each
transverse inclination is modified by a different diagonal.
The sequence of transition from
plane to plane is flat, steep,
suspended. In the peripheral
three-ring, the transition from
plane to plane is horizontal,
vertical, sagittal.

Transverse three-rings showing
the diagonal axis in each:

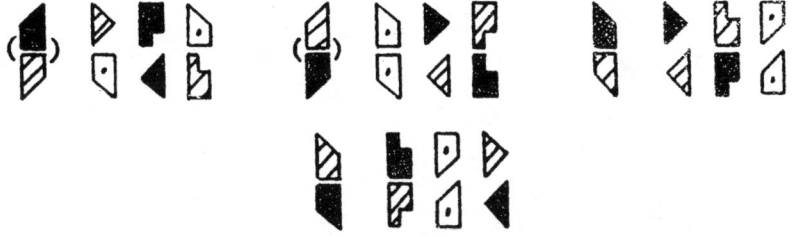

Peripheral three-rings showing
the diagonal axis in each:

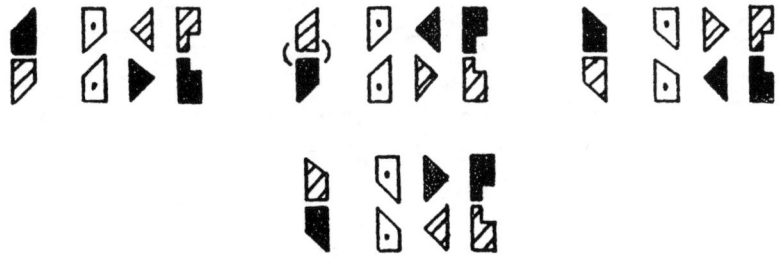

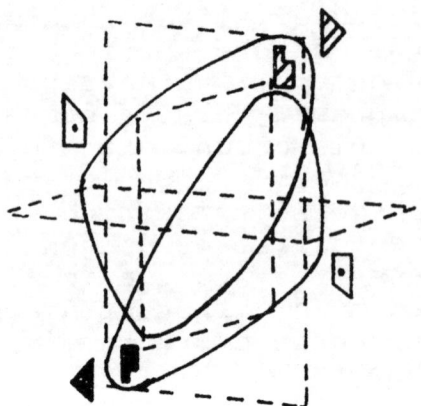

Two transverse three-rings
from diagonal

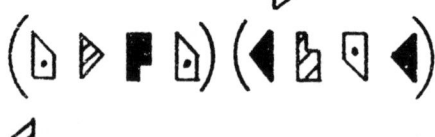

Two peripheral three-rings
around diagonal

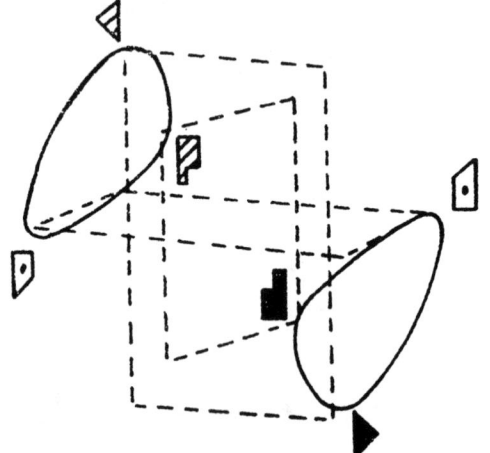

APPENDIX: DIRECTIONS IN SPACE

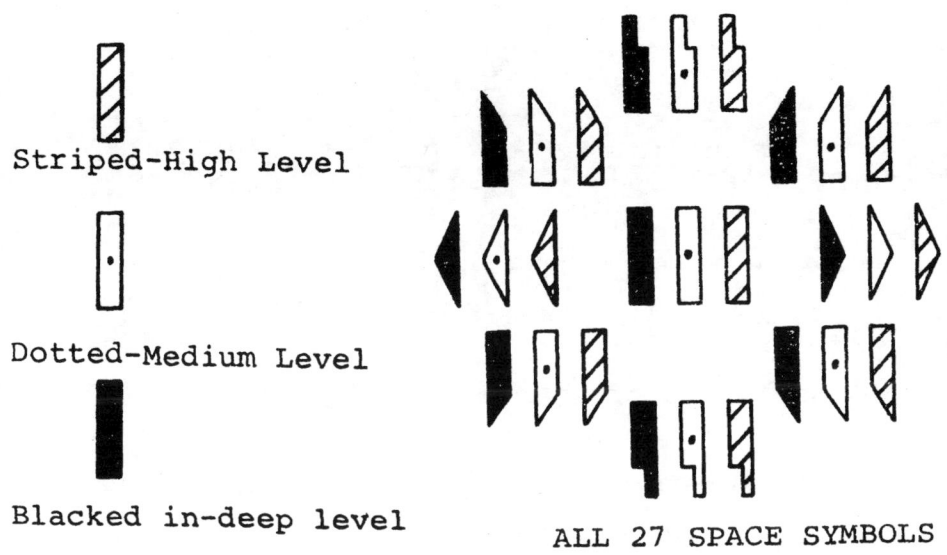

Striped-High Level

Dotted-Medium Level

Blacked in-deep level

ALL 27 SPACE SYMBOLS

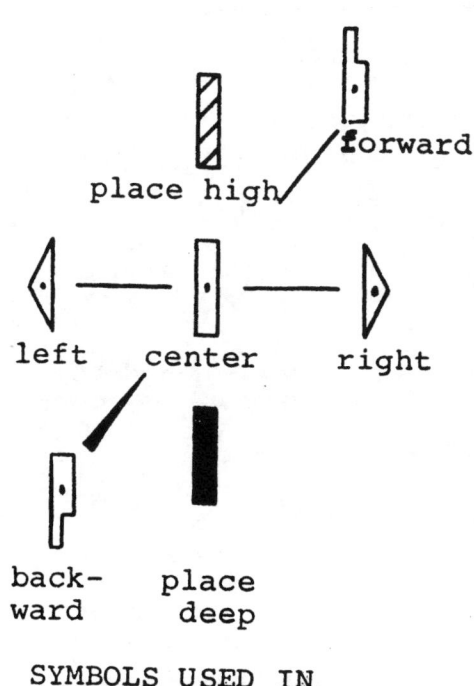

place high — forward

left — center — right

backward — place deep

SYMBOLS USED IN
OCTAHEDRON

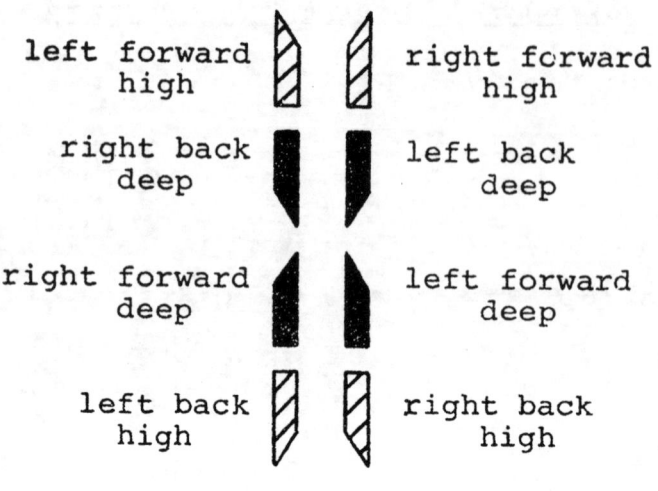

left forward high right forward high

right back deep left back deep

right forward deep left forward deep

left back high right back high

SYMBOLS USED IN CUBE

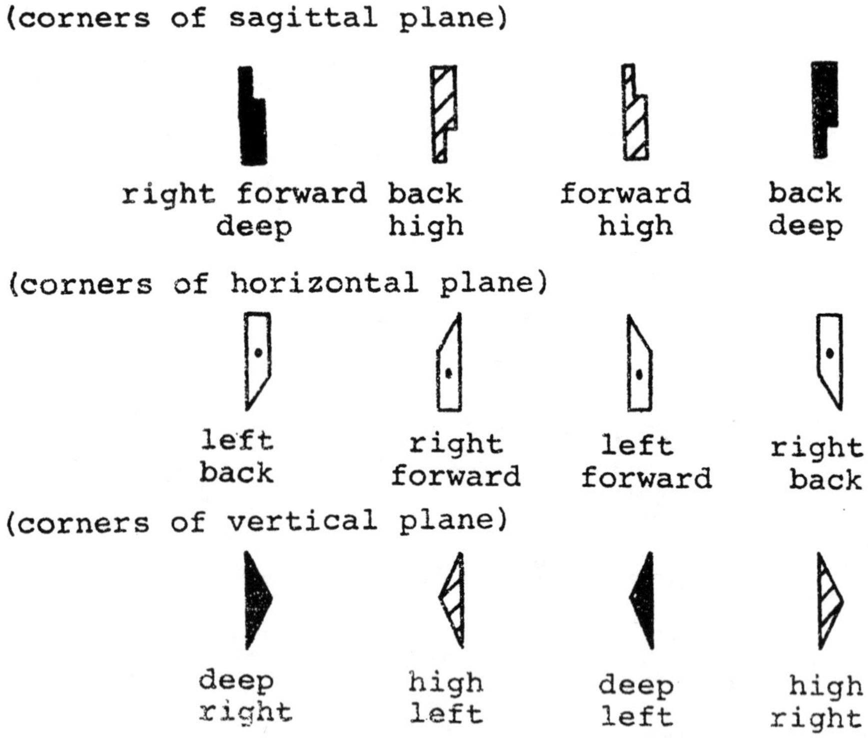

(corners of sagittal plane)

right forward deep back high forward high back deep

(corners of horizontal plane)

left back right forward left forward right back

(corners of vertical plane)

deep right high left deep left high right

SYMBOLS USED IN ICOSAHEDRON